GODS OF INDIA

Vishnu Slays the Demons

SHUBHA VILAS

Vishnu is the supreme godhead and is the protector of the entire Universe. When evil energies become strong, Vishnu swings into action and restores the balance on Earth. He lives in Vaikuntha, the divine spiritual world. His wife is Lakshmi, the most celebrated goddess of fortune.

One day, Vishnu was sleeping on his favourite bed Sheshnag, surrounded by waters of destruction on all sides. From his ear, emerged two frightful demons-Madhu and Kaitab.

They immediately sought shelter of the divine mother to empower them with boons. For one thousand years, they immersed themselves in meditation till the goddess was finally pleased with them and granted them the power of being undefeatable.

Overjoyed with their achievement, they began to explore the world around them and stumbled upon the sole living being in the Universe. It was none other than Brahmadeva, sitting serenely with his eyes closed, deeply engrossed in meditation.

Madhu and Kaitab laughed heartily when they saw his choice of seat. It was a pretty pink lotus flower, the stem of which ran all the way down connecting to Vishnu's navel. He looked so innocent and a perfect target for harassing. Moreover, they wanted to try out their skills of hacking knowledge from another's mind.

The two of them closed upon Brahma and started the process of knowledge transfer from his mind. Brahma immediately sensed an attack and his eyelids flew open. He could feel his Vedic knowledge draining out. But when he saw two towering personalities bent over him, he panicked. He was no match for the demons. He needed help!

He saw no one, not a single soul who could come to his rescue. The only one who had the power to help him was Vishnudeva. But Vishnu was in deep slumber. He tried shaking the lotus stem to bring Vishnu out of his reverie. But nothing happened.

His silent lips sent a prayerful distress call to the divine energy, Nidradevi (goddess of sleep) to reduce her effect on Vishnu and allow him to wake up. Sure enough, Nidradevi left the eyes, nostrils and chest of Vishnu.

Meanwhile, Madhu and Kaitab were done with downloading the Vedas into their memory. Then they spotted the slumbering Vishnu, looking absolutely radiant and serene. Dressed in yellow, with Kaustubhmani on his chest, there was a golden aura around him. They inched closer to have a good look. To their surprise, Vishnu suddenly opened his eyes and pierced them with his deep stare.

The demons were itching to fight someone as they had been inactive for a thousand years. A fierce battle began between Vishnu, Madhu and Kaitab. The demons fought tooth and nail, not giving Vishnu any chance to overpower them.

They jumped and rolled and flew in the air with such agility that Vishnu had to admire their fighting spirit. Even after five thousand years of fighting, the demons did not give up.

Finally it dawned on Vishnu that he would never be able to subdue them because of their boon. He changed his strategy and suggested them to ask for anything they wished from him. The puffed up demons replied that they did not want anything but they could give Vishnu whatever he wanted.

This was the opportunity Vishnu was waiting for. He immediately pounced on it and said he wanted their lives. Caught in their own trap, the demons agreed to give up their lives provided he did not kill them in water. So Vishnu used his thigh to place their heads and his Sudarshan Chakra beheaded the two demons. Vishnu is since them called Madhusudan, killer of Madhu demon.

As soon as they died, Brahma got back his knowledge of the Vedas and continued with his penance and Vishnu went back to his snake bed for a peaceful snooze. Time and again Lord Vishnu comes in various forms to the rescue whenever the demoniac influence increases and the innocent are being tormented.